Jimmy Page Adult Coloring Book

I0842135

Legendary Guitarist and Epic Rock'n'Roll Persona, Led Zeppelin Mastermind and Talent Inspired Adult Coloring Book

Carolyn Simmons

LED-ZEPPELIN

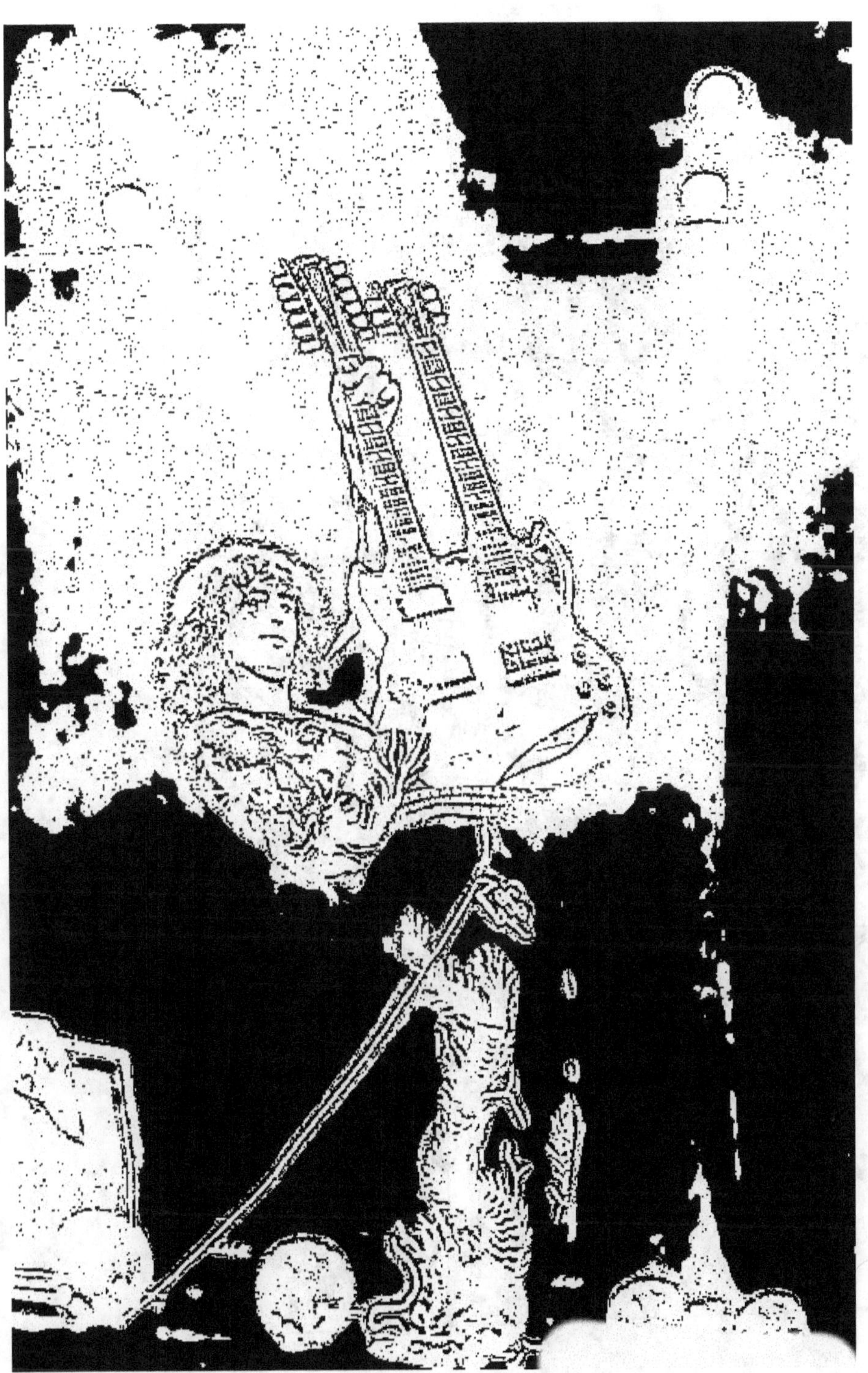

FILLMORE EAST
JAN. 1969

SEATTLE
7-17-73
LEDZEPPELIN.COM

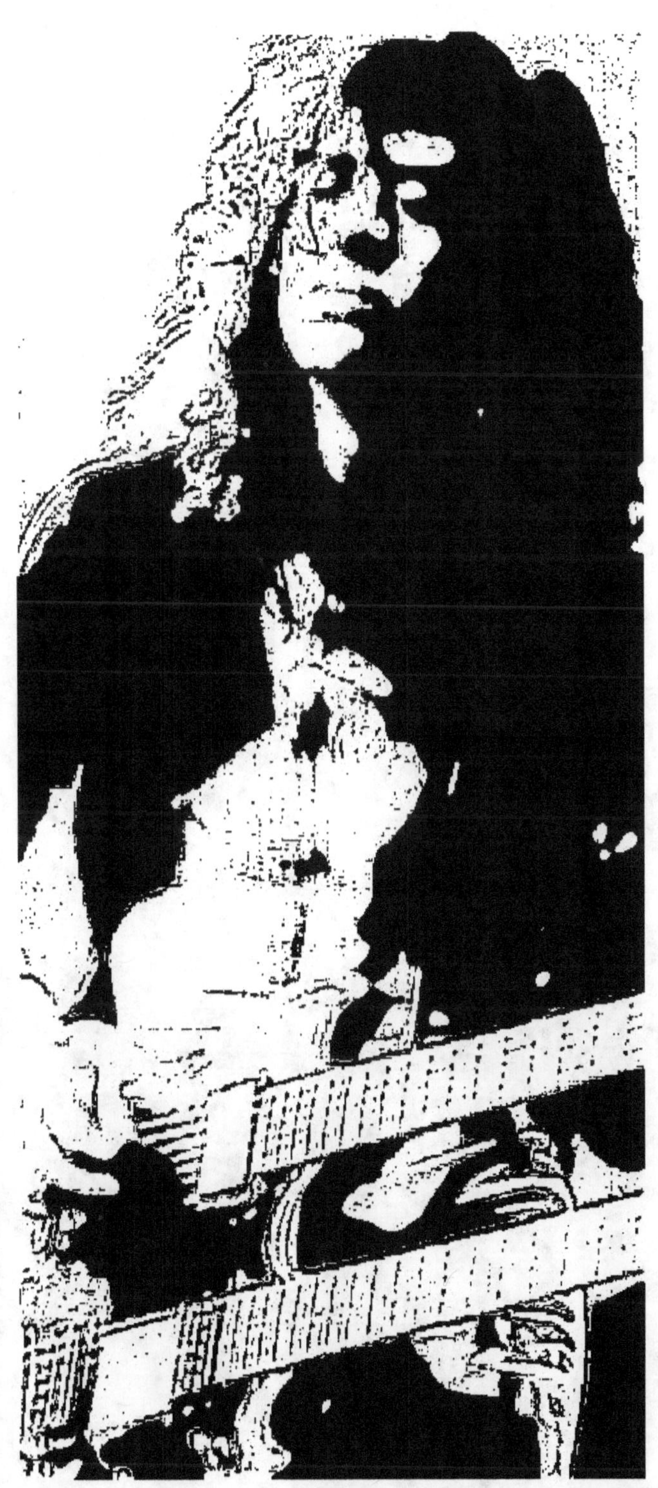

www.ingramcontent.com/pod-product-compliance
Lightning Source LLC
Chambersburg PA
CBHW051928250726
48659CB00002B/897